Your HIRE Calling:

Unconventional Job Search Tactics That Work For College Students in ANY Economy

by Joe Mayne

Book design by Nichole Ward, Morrison Alley Design

Although the author and publisher have made every effort to ensure the accuracy and completeness of information contained in this book, we assume no responsibility for errors, inaccuracies, omissions, or any inconsistency herein. Any slights of people, places, or organizations are unintentional.

First Printing 2009

ISBN 978-0-9841687-0-5

This book is dedicated to my family and friends
who challenge me to keep on climbing.

TABLE OF CONTENTS

Acknowledgments

Many thanks go out to thousands of students whose energy and passion provide sustenance to me. And to all of my brothers in Delta Sigma Pi. Their example for excellence and service to others has given me a template that I attempt to follow. Thanks to all of you.

Introduction

Over the past 15 years, I've had the opportunity to work with literally thousands of college students and new graduates. And what I've found, year after year and class after class, is that young people entering the workforce almost always have the same concerns: they all want to graduate from school and get a great job that pays lots of money. What I've also learned, though, is that the best ways to do that have changed over time.

For one thing, a lot of the old tried and true tactics aren't working as well as they used to. Because so many of today's young people have read the same books, and gotten all the same advice, they end up coming across as very professional, but virtually indistinguishable from one another. By following all the standard rules, they make it harder for employers to notice them and decide that they're the right ones to hire.

At the same time, technology is changing the way we look for work– as well as the way we're hired. Where ten years ago it was more difficult for a prospective employer to find out about a prospective employee, and the only real option to find out about people was to undergo an extensive background search through a private investigator, that same information can now be found simply by going online. The amount of data that exists about individuals online, especially on social networking sites like Facebook, MySpace, and LinkedIn, has changed the way employers check out their prospective hires.

And finally, the economy is changing not only the way that students look for jobs, but their expectations of what they'll find. During the late 90s, it wasn't uncommon for me to hear new graduates talking about salaries, vacation schedules, and stock option packages. In today's tough economy, however, young people are wiser. They realize that graduates – who have no track record or experience – can be lucky to get jobs in the first place.

Within all of this change and chaos, my presentations have changed over the years. My advice to students, however, has been fairly consistent. That's because, when it's all said and done, there are always going to be jobs for those candidates who can manage to stand out. No amount of economic turmoil or global competition is ever going to change that. The world needs fresh faces and companies need new employees. That's a theme that I'm going to come back to time and again in this short book, and it's one you would do well to remember. The job market can be daunting sometimes, but never forget that it exists because every company, big or small, in every corner of the world, needs people just like you. The trick is showing prospective employers that you're the right person for their very best openings.

Luckily, that's what I've been teaching for more than a decade. In my work as a manager and recruiter, I've seen firsthand what employers want. Often, after I share that insight in a campus presentation, I receive lots of letters, e-mails, and phone calls from the students I've spoken to. Some of them have gone on to great jobs, while others tell me how excited they are to get started on their job search armed with this inside information. But most of all, they ask me if there isn't a way to take all of the advice I've given them and use it going forward. For a long time, I didn't have a good answer. Until I finally found the time to put what I've learned into this book. It isn't just a collection of job hunting tips – it's the kind of insight I wish I'd had when I started my career.

At the time, I was a young man looking for a good job with a well-known company, but I didn't know the first thing about how to go about finding it. Luckily, when a recruiter from a Fortune 500 company called one of my marketing professors, he gave my name as a recommendation. Since then, I've learned that my stroke of luck, rare as it was, wasn't an accident. There are dozens of things that students and graduates can do to set themselves apart from the competition and ensure that they'll get the best chance to be hired.

In the following chapters you'll find tools and tips to make sure that you stand out and not only get a job, but secure a first stepping stone in your career. Notice, though, that I didn't promise that you will get your dream job. Very few young people can graduate from school and step immediately into a position that they would still want, or expect to be working at, a few years later. Besides, most of them wouldn't be ready for it even if they could. I'll talk about this at greater length later on the book, but I want to start you off with the right expectations. As someone who's leaving a two or four-year institution, you should expect that you're going to be able to find a great job with a great company that's going to allow you to grow your career. Is that to say that you'll make six figures right away, or that you'll spend seven weeks out of the year at your beach house in Maui? Of course not. But if you can follow the advice in this book, you can put yourself well onto that path – or any other that you like.

With that in mind, I'm going to make you two promises. The first is that everything you'll find in these pages works. In my time evaluating students and graduates as a recruiter, I've had the opportunity to interview more than two thousand young people. What's more, my research in this field has put me in touch with hundreds of other hiring managers, along with students and college placement staff. I have studied the problem of getting noticed and hired from all the angles, so you can be confident that I'm pointing you in the right direction.

My second promise is that I won't waste your time. You'll notice that this is one of the shorter titles on job hunting you'll ever read, and there's a good reason for that. The simple fact that you picked up this book tells me that you're serious about finding a job and starting a career. And if that's true, I know you're busy enough as it is. Not only do you have to worry about finding a job, but you might be struggling to keep up with classes, finals, part-time work, sports, and other activities – not to mention spending a few moments with the friends who've been there with you for the past few years. That's why, in these pages, you're not going to find a lot of academic or philosophical discussions. I wanted to write something that would be straight to the point – something you could use right away to improve your job search.

With those points out of the way, let's get started on finding you the job you deserve. Remember, no matter what's going on in the world, companies are hiring. They're trying desperately to find someone just like you – all you have to do is make yourself easy to find.

Chapter 1

Don't Start Here

Do we really need another book about job hunting?

That was the question I put to myself as I started to compile the notes and outlines that became the title you're holding in your hands right now. After all, we're living in a time when today's students are savvier than ever. In visiting campuses over the past decade and a half, I've been continually impressed by how much young people know about jobs, careers, and how to get them. Most of you are already aware, for example, of how to format a resume and tie a Windsor knot; and if you don't, there are a hundred other places where you could find that information. You've all learned the basics already. What you might not know, though, is that the basics aren't enough to get you a job.

In the same way that each Olympics seems to bring faster and stronger athletes breaking one record after another, modern graduates have outdone themselves to the point where simply being an outstanding candidate isn't enough – you need to sit head and shoulders above all the other job seekers out there just to get noticed. Because all the other young men and women you're competing against have read the same books and websites you have, they know to dress the same way and give the same answers. What you need is an inside edge, and I'm going to give it to you.

But in the process, I'm going to assume some things. For instance, I'm going to take it as a given that you already know what a resume is and how to go about putting one together. Likewise, I'm not going to bother telling you that you should dress like a professional and try to keep your grades above a failing level. There are lots of great titles out there on basic job search skills, and I recommend that you check lots of them out. What I'm going to do is add on to what you've learnt. I've seen more than ten thousand resumes and interviewed more than two thousand candidates just like you – I want to show you what recruiters and managers are thinking when you're sitting across the table from them, not tell you to firm up your handshake.

So, if you are just starting out, or if you aren't sure you have the basics down, then go ahead and take the time to bring yourself up to speed. There are a lot of great texts out there on how to put together a resume, dress for success, look for a job on the Internet, and so on. You can find dozens of them online, at your local bookstore, or at your campus retailer.

I've even included a suggested reading list in the back of this book to get you started.

In fact, you should make sure to take advantage of the other resources available to you, whether they're in print or not. This will be a common theme throughout this book, but one that bears repeating several times. College students and recent graduates have a distinct advantage over almost every other job seeker out there, if for no other reason than they have access to some of the top minds and resources for finding a job. Take a moment to consider all of the options there are for you.

For one thing, you have access to your professors. In nearly every field of study, the instructors come from a working background. Most likely, these men and women have gotten to where they are because they've already been through what you're about to do. They worked in the industry, met the people, and done the work. When it comes to finding the way in, they're perfect guides. I've met very few professors who aren't willing to help their students, but sadly, they aren't asked nearly as often as they should be.

Your friends and family can be a great resource, too. Again, this is an area where lots of students overlook the obvious, but your parents, uncles and aunts, cousins, all might have been through this process before. Don't be shy about asking them for advice, recommendations, or even referrals. They want you to succeed, and best of all, no one expects a new graduate to have a job. That puts you in a great position, because the people in your life are going to expect that you're going to ask them for help when you need it. Unlike the executive who has been laid off after twenty years, you're surrounded by people who realize that you're going to want their assistance in finding employment, and so they're going to be open to pitching in.

Don't overlook your campus career placement center, either. Almost every college I go to has one, and they're usually staffed by some of the smartest and most helpful people you'll ever meet. These people are experts in helping you become employed, and they can help you every step of the way. Much of what I teach people about resumes, interviewing, etc., can be sharpened by continual work with them. And remember, it's never too early to stop in; freshmen and sophomores are welcome. Even though you might not be looking for a job yet, there's nothing to say you can't start preparing your materials. So, if you haven't been your campus career placement center, put down this book and stop in today.

So, while this might be the last book you'll ever need on the subject of getting a job, I sincerely hope it's not your first. Think of these chapters like you would a sprinkle of cinnamon or chocolate on the top of a cappuccino. On their own, they would be a bit bitter, and not really enough to drink. But added to the hot coffee and milk that's already there, they can turn something ordinary into a fantastic treat.

I've written this book for three different types of people:

First, there are the students and recent graduates who are entering the workforce, or will be soon. These are the young men and women who need to get a job now, and rest assured, everything you'll find in the following chapters will be aimed at helping you along that goal. Today's job market is more competitive than ever, and at the time of this writing, the economy is putting on added pressure. That doesn't mean that there aren't jobs out there. The fact of the matter is that there are literally thousands of companies, small and large and in every part of the country, who are looking to add new employees. No organization can grow, or even maintain, without adding new talent to their staff.

What's more, they love college students and recent graduates for a few reasons. For one thing, they come cheaper than other employees. Someone who's established in their field might command a salary that's two or three times what a recent graduate can earn, so the young represent great value for the investment. More than that, there's the fact that young people tend to bring more energy and enthusiasm to the job than can be found elsewhere. They know technology, they're aware of what's new, and they breathe a breath of fresh air into every company. Keep that in mind as you begin your job search – employers need you.

The second audience for this book is students who aren't yet graduating or looking for employment. While your needs might not be as immediate, your opportunities are even greater. Why do I say that? Because a lot of the strategies outlined in this book work best over time. Someone who has three years to devote to their job search has a distinct advantage over someone who has three months. The simple fact you don't need a job today means that you can do all of the things that many students will wish they had done when they were in your shoes. These include building items on your resume, gaining professional and social experience, and practicing for the interview.

So, if you're an underclassman, I urge you to flip through these pages, make some notes, and get started today. Then, as time goes on, you can refer back to this text from time to time, or visit my website at www.maynespeaker.com, to keep finding fresh ideas. By the time your graduation comes, you might not even have to look for a job. The strategies I'm going to show you are so effective that I've seen recruiters seek out students before they even had a chance to put together their resumes.

And finally, this book is for the parents, friends, relatives, professors, and job career center staff who support our young people as they branch out and begin their careers. By studying the tips and tools I'm going to give you, and learning the mindset of a recruiter, you can gather advice that goes far beyond what was available when you and I were going through this process. I encourage you to read this book, pass along, or even buy additional copies for the students in your life, because it can give them an advantage that will last a lifetime.

The Basics Are Really Important

Just because I'm not teaching you the basics of job searching, that doesn't mean they aren't important. Film director Woody Allen once said that "90% of success is just showing up." There's a lot of truth to that, at least when it comes to your quest to find an open position. A great many candidates fail to "show up" for the top positions because they don't understand or learn about the simplest parts of the process. They send out resumes that don't follow accepted styles, for example, or ones that have persistent typos and errors. They fail to learn about interview etiquette, and so they show up looking unprofessional. Each of these errors disqualifies them for the best jobs right off the bat. I don't want you to make the same mistake.

Treat your search for employment like you would one of your hardest classes. Study up, hit the books, and take the time to compare notes with your friends. Finding a job is a lot harder than just sending a few e-mails or putting qualifications down in a word processing program. But if you don't even have the right tools to start with, nothing I can teach you is going to make any difference. To succeed, you are going to have to know the right way to look for a job, as well as the accepted methods for presenting yourself.

One point that you'll come across a few times in this book is that there is such a thing as too much common sense. After all, there's a reason it's so common. If you strictly follow every convention, take every piece of advice you've read in a book to heart, and act the way they tell you to act all the time, you're going to blend in with every other student. That's not an advantage to you. In fact, it may leave the recruiter with the feeling that you're just another face in the crowd. So how do you know when you should blend in, and when it's okay to try to stand out?

The answer comes with knowledge and experience. You can't ever know which rules are okay to break until you've learned what the rules are and why they are there in the first place. As you begin to understand the job hunting process, you'll discover the benefits of letting your true self come through, while at the same time not being so outrageous that you seem like a hiring risk. Walking that fine line isn't as difficult as you think, and throughout these chapters I'm going to show you a number of ways that you can stand out while still seeming like a professional. This book is all about going beyond the basics, but you can't do that without spending the time to learn them first.

Chapter 2

Finding Your Place

Who are you going to be when you graduate? A lot of students I talk to don't really take the time to consider this question as deeply as they should. I can understand why; there are always a million and two things going on around any college campus. Besides classes and clubs, there are jobs, friends, and dozens of other distractions that can keep them from looking at the big picture.

But when you really think about it, going to college isn't just about earning a degree — it's about positioning yourself to become the future "you" you want to be. And as busy as you are, being in school offers the best chance most people are ever going to get to figure that out. Because even if you don't have the slightest clue, you're surrounded by professors, job counselors, and other professionals who can at least get you started asking the right questions.

So, the first thing to do before you even begin your job search is to think about what kind of position or career you want to get started in. Try to take what I call "the 30,000 foot view" of your life and look over the terrain and into the horizon. Don't focus on any details; just take some time to consider who you are, what you enjoy, and where you see yourself a few years down the road. If you feel overwhelmed by thoughts or questions, start scribbling down on a piece of paper. The point isn't to do something that's incredibly structured, it's to start thinking about where you want to end up when your time at school ends.

Don't limit yourself to professional ambitions. It's great to put a finger on what kind of job you want to have, or what salary range you see yourself in, but go deeper. Try to envision where you'd want to live, and what kind of lifestyle you'll be enjoying. Would you be at the office a lot, or the kind of person who has the freedom to work from home? What about travel, weekends, or time with your family? Forming a picture of the future you want might not seem like such a big deal now, and you seem to have so little control over it, but it can pay enormous dividends later.

As you start to go through this process, don't be afraid to ask for help. If you don't know how many hours the average sales manager puts in, or what a reasonable paycheck for an experienced accountant looks like, find a friend or relative who does. Or, if you just don't know anyone, then go ahead and reach out to a stranger. People are generally great about giving advice to students. They all want to help you avoid the traps and pitfalls they came across, and so they'll give you some of their time as long as you don't abuse the privilege.

Besides, talking to some folks on the outside is a great way to reconcile your hopes and dreams with the real world. You're very likely to find that, within the career and lifestyle that you're thinking of, there are trade-offs and compromises to be made. Maybe one type of job offers a great salary, while another doesn't pay as much but gives you the flexibility to set your own hours. Only you can decide which of those is worth more to you, but it's a good idea to go into your career knowing what those decisions will look like.

When you've got a picture in your mind of what your future job and life might look like, start to work backwards. Suppose you're planning to be a top sales producer for a Fortune 500 firm, or a human resources director in the Pacific Northwest. That's a good starting point, but what job would come before that? Often, the job you really want is two or three promotions from what you can get as a new graduate, but that shouldn't deter you. Most students don't enter the real world and get their dream jobs right away (more on this in a moment) so don't try to aim for that target. Instead, look to map out a flowchart of where you want to go, and then see where you can jump in. An entry-level job is just that — an entry. Use it to your advantage by making it an entry into something you want to do.

What to do when you don't know what to do.

Suppose you don't know what you want to do when you graduate? Is that a big deal? Well, that depends; if you've still got two years to figure it out, then I wouldn't lose sleep over it. If, on the other hand, you're getting your diploma in the next few weeks, I'll understand if your lack of career direction is giving you heartburn. Don't let it get you too knotted up, though. You're definitely not the first person to be in that position and you'll come out of it just fine.

The first step, whether you've got several semesters or just a few hours to figure things out, is to start with your interests. Everyone has something they like to do, even if it's just a hobby. Sometimes just thinking about *why* you enjoy those activities – you're a people person, you like computers, books are your passion, etc. – can spur you into thinking of a possible career choice.

If that doesn't yield any answers, or if you're still looking for more information, then do what I've been recommending all along: talk to the dozens of people who are eager to help you. Ask your friends and family for advice, get in touch with alumni, visit your professors, and by all means, stop by your campus career placement center. Any of these folks can shed light on the choices they've made, good and bad. And better yet, they can give you an outside perspective on yourself, helping you see your personality and talents from another point of view.

As with everything else, the Internet can be a wonderful source of information and ideas. These days, you can find more than ever about what jobs are available, which industries are in growth, the pay ranges and advancement potential for various positions, and so on. You shouldn't use websites as your only source of information, but they can be a great place to start.

Once you start to get some ideas, or even if you don't, make a point of visiting a few companies. One of the fastest ways to find out what you think of a job, and whether you'd enjoy it, is to spend a day with someone who's working in the field. Find someone who's gotten the kind of job you're looking at, and simply ask them how they like it. See if they'd mind you stopping by for a couple of hours to see what an actual working day is like. Most employers won't mind, and you get two big benefits: first, you get an actual real-life test drive of the career choice you're considering. At the same time, you make valuable acquaintances within the company. If you decide it might be the profession for you, you'll be more prepared to interview because you know the right questions to ask and qualifications to display. You might even get to know people who could recommend you to recruiters, or the hiring managers themselves.

Like many of the strategies in this book, the earlier you start the better, because by the time you graduate you want to have a more or less fully formed idea of what kind of job you're looking for and where you can get it. You don't have to have it all figured out by the time you don your cap and gown, but it sure helps.

With that being said, though, don't freak out if you just can't decide. There are lots of people, even in their 40s, 50s, and 60s, who still haven't figured out what they want to do when they grow up. Sometimes the absence of a set plan inspires them to take risks and try new things that end up being wildly successful. As long as you follow the tips in this book, you're going to be infinitely more employable than most of your peers, and you can always change career paths if things don't work out.

If that's the case with you, then focus on things you're interested in, combined with the lifestyle factors that are important to you. If you know already what part of the country you want to live in, how many hours a week you want to work, or what salary is important to you, then you can create a starting point. From there, you can get a job that will take you places in a few years, without the pressure warning about the rest of your life.

Come to think of it, that's good advice for anyone who's looking into their future. Remember that the next page on the calendar is full of unknowns, and don't get so focused on the endgame that you miss the forest for the trees. Most of us, once we enter the working world, find that our hopes, dreams, and desires start to evolve. What looked good when we were sophomores seems a bit bland once we're in the working world. Or, we find that we have new interests that haven't been discovered yet.

One interesting facet of our hypercompetitive, fast-paced, global economy is that there are entirely new jobs and industries springing up all the time. Some of the best jobs you can get today – like a web development engineer, or the logistics coordinator for a data website – didn't exist as possibilities fifteen or twenty years ago. No one had even thought of them, much less majored in them or considered them a viable career path. For that reason, you shouldn't get too attached to any one notion of what you'd like your future to be like. No one knows what tomorrow will bring, but you might find the charger on along a completely different path than you originally envisioned.

Hopefully, this chapter has gotten you started on thinking about where you'd like to end up after you graduate – even if you're not sure where your ultimate career destination lies – because we're going to spend the following chapters positioning you as the ultimate, up and coming professional candidate for that field. It's going to involve some work and effort, but I can promise you that it's going to be worth it when you get the job you've been planning to take for years, while many of your colleagues are forced to settle for the first thing that comes along.

Getting Your First Job, Not Your Dream Job

In one survey after another, I've found that students' greatest fears aren't that they won't get a job when they finish school – it's that they'll get one that they can't stand. To me, this is all part of that wonderful evolution of understanding that I've been talking about; rather than just look to get a stable job like their grandparents did, today's graduates anticipate that they're going to have multiple careers, and so they see the big picture. They don't want a paycheck and a pension… they want the whole experience.

I think that's fantastic, but I'm going to say something now that might seem like a slap in the face to a lot of you. Here's the cold, hard truth: your first job is not going to be your dream job. And what's more, it shouldn't be.

Let me explain that a bit. I have worked with lots of young people over the years, and I've noticed something interesting along the way. With each graduation class, the new job seekers have come in knowing more about working life than ever before. Unlike their grandparents, who went into the workforce blind, worked hard, and hoped to retire with a gold watch, they hate the thought of slaving away at a meaningless, low-paid job. I don't want that for you either, but I think it's important that you go into the job hunting process with realistic expectations. Most jobs for graduates are entry-level, meaning just that — they are a place to start. You can use them as stepping stones to bigger things, but you shouldn't expect them to be all that fulfilling — socially, intellectually, or financially — all by themselves.

Believe it or not, that's okay, because you probably wouldn't be ready for your dream job yet, anyway — if you even know what it is. A first job is a chance for a company to get to know about you, but also should be a chance for you to get to know about them and yourself. As I said, most people realize sometime after they graduate that their needs have changed. They don't want the things they thought they wanted at all, and so they're forced to reevaluate. By not setting your expectations sky high for your first job out of college, you're creating space to grow and evaluate.

Please don't take this advice to mean that you should settle for anything. I think a lot of graduates sell themselves short, or take the job that pays the most at the outset, despite the fact that it doesn't offer much in the way of growth, or isn't in the field they wanted to work in. That's a big mistake. A stepping stone is only as good as the next step it takes you to. No job that you're going to get right out of college is worth it if it doesn't offer advancement somewhere else. So, keep your eyes open and know what you're getting into.

Chapter 3

Leveraging Campus Life

Job searching is a bit like studying for a major exam. You can make things easy on yourself by preparing in little bits, day after day, for a long period of time, or you can give yourself an ulcer by cramming at the last minute and hoping for the best. Is it possible that you could do all that studying and still not get a good grade, or that you could glance at the material for a few minutes the night before and somehow ace the test? Sure, but one is the much safer path to success, and you shouldn't gamble with your future opportunities.

There are all kinds of things you can do while you're in college to improve your chances of having a great job lined up by the time you graduate. The best part is, none of them are difficult. You don't have to do anything miraculous to position yourself as an up and coming professional, or in most cases, even leave campus. All you have to do is start adding to the picture of yourself as the perfect candidate

– one piece here, one piece there, until they make such a compelling case that recruiters can't help but notice.

Maybe the easiest way is to do well in your classes, although my definition of doing well and yours might be different. To me, the great student is the one who gets good grades, but doesn't obsess about having a 4.0 GPA. They're more concerned about being involved in class discussions, participating in group activities, and learning the material. As I mentioned earlier, I got my first job – a great position with a Fortune 500 company – because one of my professors recommended me. He didn't think of my name, however, because I got straight A's or because I had the sharpest mind in the room. No, he thought of me because he knew I was someone who was competent and genuinely interested in what I was learning about. I wouldn't have been able to make that impression if I was faking it, but I really enjoyed the material we were going through. This goes back to what I brought up in the last chapter; I picked a major that I liked and it showed.

More specifically, though, I set myself apart from the other students in my class because of my energy and enthusiasm. I didn't think much about it at the time, but after many years spent in the business world, and thousands of hours on the other side of the interviewer's desk, I've come to realize that what I was doing generally goes by a simple name – branding.

When I first bring up the topic of branding with college students, they are sometimes surprised. They remember reading about it for marketing class, but they don't always see immediately what it has to do with their efforts to get a job. But what I've learned, and try to explain, is the same thing that multinational corporations have spent billions of dollars to figure out: that people buy brands. They don't look for denim jeans, or soft drinks, or sneakers; they try to find a unique product that stands out above all others in the marketplace. They look for the one thing that seems to be jumping off the shelf at them.

Recruiters are no different. When they look through a stack of resumes, or put questions to one job candidate after another, they're trying to make the best buying decisions for themselves and their companies. But what they really want isn't a new employee, it's the one new hire who will bring a burst of talent, energy, and enthusiasm into their business or department. They're looking for the graduate who seems to jump off the shelf at them. It's your job to be that young man or woman.

Building your brand starts a long time before your interview, however. In fact, it even begins well before you've put the first letter of your first name on your resume. That's because your personal brand is a reputation. It's the sum of what you look like to a prospective employer; what they should expect if they hire you. Your goal is to create a brand and image of yourself as the ideal employee – smart, hard-working, and a team player. You can leverage your time on campus, bit by bit, to grow an impression that does just that.

The first step is to simply go beyond your classes and get involved, especially with the professional clubs and associations available in and out of your major. Few things will help you stand out in a recruiter's mind more than your membership in these kinds of groups. When you join the marketing club, the accounting group, or engineering society, for example, it tells prospective employers a lot of things: that you're interested in what you're doing, that you're able to work with other people, and that you're always learning new things. Also, the meetings and events you attend are going to give you the opportunity to meet lots of people working in your field of study. This makes the time you spend valuable by itself because they can help you expand your knowledge about the industry. Plus, you get used to being around the kinds of men and women you'd be working with in the real world. And finally, these are people who are going have staffing needs down the road, or know others who do.

You might also look at getting involved in your community. In every town and city anywhere in the world, there are people who need help. There's never a bad time to pitch in, but it's especially beneficial when you're young. For one thing, it can help you keep your own problems and struggles in perspective. Few things can make you appreciate what you have in this world as getting a firsthand look at the challenges that others are facing every day. Empathy is an important career skill, and one that makes you a better all around human being.

In a perfect world, doing things for charity would be its own reward, and if you try it, you may indeed find that you'll continue it for that reason. But, I should point out that employers love students who volunteer because it shows that they're compassionate people, and that they have interests that lie beyond themselves. The best employees are team players; helping out on your own time demonstrates that you're able to work with others, see the big picture, and are willing to pitch in.

Professional fraternities are a great idea, as well, because they combine business ties with community work. When I was in school, I was a member of the business organization Delta Sigma pi, and it's been a big boost to my career even to this day. I met all kinds of future leaders, made contacts within different industries, and got some early experience as an organizational leader, each of which was important to me when I graduated. And, as part of our membership, we were encouraged to help out in different community causes from time to time. In that way, my time with the group did double duty, helping me to round out a few parts of my personal brand at once. I strongly encourage you to talk to the members of similar organizations on your campus. Beyond the job hunting advantages I've already mentioned, they're a great place to make lifelong friends.

The power of your personal brand is magnified by the number of people who hear about you as a possible employee. For some strange reason, though, most students never turn to the handful of people who are in the best position to help them out – their professors. Never overlook your instructors as a possible resource. They've already been out in the working world; they can offer advice and contacts that can make your job search much easier than it would be if you were doing everything on your own.

Of course, you shouldn't turn to your professors if you've been a terrible student, but don't assume that they won't help you out just because you didn't score perfectly on every test you took. Like employment recruiters, they know that the real value of a student goes far beyond their grades. They'll be eager to help out a student who has shown a strong interest in their coursework, so don't be shy about asking them for tips or direction. Or, if you're just getting started in your core courses, try to become the kind of student your professors would recommend. Speak up in class, do your work, and let them know that you're appreciative of their help. Show the effort and they'll remember, just as my professor did.

The object of all these steps isn't just to make your years on campus more fulfilling, although it will do that. It's also about leveraging your time to build momentum. That's because, professionally speaking, you show up to college as a nobody. No one has ever heard of you, and you don't have any skills or resources that would make you employable for a professional position in the real world. But by taking classes, working with associations, and developing the business and social skills you need to integrate into a company, you're doing the groundwork needed to get a job. If you go the extra step and start to make contact with people and build yourself as a professional instead of student, then you start to add to your weight as a job candidate. Do enough of this, and sooner or later you're in a different league than the other young men and women you're graduating with. Employers will be able to know right away that you are different kind of candidate, and will treat you differently throughout the interview process.

The best way to start your career is by building your personal brand before it ever begins. Follow the advice in this chapter and employers will see you as a product that's simply too good to pass up.

Your Network Will Sustain You

Contrary to popular belief, the most valuable thing you leave college with isn't your diploma – it's that list of names in your database or contact manager. Studies and surveys show that a full 90% of new graduates find employment through referrals. What that means to you is that your focus should be on the people you can meet in your personal, academic, and professional associations, not on websites like monster.com or careerbuilder.com.

Building a strong list of names isn't as easy as shaking a few hands, however. People are going to need to see you repeatedly before they'll feel comfortable recommending you to their friends and associates, much less hiring you themselves. What's more, you need to be sure that the impression they have of you is a positive one. For that reason, you should take care to always be ready to meet people. You don't have to put on a suit and tie to grab the mail, but try not to live in sweatpants, either. You never know when you're going to run into someone who has the inside scoop on a top entry level job. When you meet them, and you will, you want to leave them with the impression that you're someone they could imagine doing great things, not just another college kid.

You should also try to put math on your side. Consider this: every professor, alumni member, advisor, and other professional contact you meet probably knows at least a hundred people in their same industry — and most will know several times that. By striking up a professional friendship with them, you don't just learn from their experience; you make them want to see you succeed. When graduation time comes, these men and women can open doors for you that you might not have even known existed.

Learning to become an effective networker doesn't have to take a lot of time or money. Simply invest in an address book or download a software package, and start to add the names of people you meet. Try to find a reason to be in touch every few months or so. You don't have to do much; just remember to send out handwritten thank you cards, pass along an article that might be of interest, or invite them out for a cup of coffee. The key isn't to overwhelm them, it's to remind them that you're still around and working on your education. By the time you graduate, you're going to seem a seasoned professional with a huge database of contacts. Get those folks thinking about job openings and you can probably generate dozens of job offers if you've done it right — I've seen students who have.

Chapter 4

Warming Your Resume

When I give a presentation to a campus audience, one of the things that I always offer to the attendees is my High Impact Resume Evaluation (H I RE) service. Basically, this is where I allow students to send me copies of their resumes and get a free professional opinion. It's one of the most rewarding parts of my job, since it allows me to work directly with young people who are just getting started in the business world, but it also prompts the greatest number of questions and inquiries I receive.

For the most part, they center around how a certain qualification should be worded, or the best way to explain a student's involvement in one activity or another. Those things are important, and I always address them. But right now, I want to make a point that many new job seekers tend to overlook: that your resume can only get you an interview. No matter what it says, it's nothing more than a foot in the door, so you should use it as such.

With that in mind, I don't think the look or wording of a resume is quite as important as how "warm" it is. By that I mean, does your resume spark an emotional connection with recruiters? If they pick it up and look it over, do you come across as just another candidate, or someone they would like to sit down and spend half an hour or forty five minutes with?

The whole trick to understanding the concept lies in seeing things from the employer's point of view. Lots of students get hung up on trying to "stack" their resumes with one qualification after another. They feel like it's important to list every skill possible, and so they end up writing descriptions of themselves that read like hardware catalogs. Given that nearly all resumes are scanned electronically these days, it *is* important to list the core skills that matter in your industry. Beyond that, though, they're probably not going to help themselves as much as they think they are.

The reason for that is that most entry-level job candidates come in with very similar skill sets. The fact that you're graduating from college tells recruiters that you can probably operate a computer, add up numbers on a spreadsheet, and so on. Aren't there other skills you're going to need on the job? You can be sure there will be, but most of them can't be learned at your school. That's because the bulk of most people's jobs have to be learned during in-house training. Employers know this; they're not expecting you to show these skills on day one. They're more concerned about whether you're the type of person who *will* learn, and will contribute to their team without causing problems.

So, rather than specific skills, what a recruiter really wants to see is an indication that you have the right attitude for work. Nearly every hiring manager I've ever met is looking for the same thing – the candidate who displays a quiet confidence and willingness to pitch in and be a team player. Everything else, from how fast they type to where they graduated in their class, is secondary. They just want someone who is going to be a good fit for their company.

How do you accomplish this? I always tell people to start with their objective line. Rather than use something bland and generic, let it reflect the type of work and responsibilities that will be a part of your new employer's job. I mentioned in the first chapter that following the common wisdom can sometimes leave you coming up short. This is one of those areas. Lots of students make the mistake of taking their objectives straight from a book. Again, there's nothing wrong with this on the surface. The problem, though, comes in when you consider that thousands of other students are doing the same thing, making your resume seem like everyone else's. For example, and stop me if this sounds familiar, I'm seeing a lot of young people lately who are "looking for an exciting job with the fast-paced company that will take advantage of their work ethic and ambition."

Thousands of resumes, one after another, have used a line just like that on the cover. It was probably great the first time (back in the Stone Age), but has little effect today. A better approach is to write something specific and detailed. For instance, if your big desire is to see the world, why not highlight that fact? Open your resume with something like "I'm looking for a position that will take advantage of my strong interest in travel and international business."

Now, if you're saying to yourself, "but I might not get the job with an objective like that," then the problem isn't with your objective – it's with the kind of job you're applying for. If the two aren't in sync, you're only setting yourself up for failure. Because if you're applying for jobs that don't match up to your real ambitions, one of two things is going to happen: you are either going to get a job that you don't like, or you're not going to get one at all because you seem like all the other recent graduates. Make sure your objective says something about who you are and what you really want. It will just give recruiters a warmer sense of who you are; it can also help you end up in a position that actually furthers your career.

Another way to get an emotional response from your resume is by taking advantage of all of those memberships and programs that I advised you to participate in. Listing on your resume that you have done volunteer work, or that you spent several semesters helping out with the business fraternity or professional organization, tells the recruiter that you're probably someone who gets along with others. And don't hesitate to include some of your activities from high school. For most college students, that wasn't so long ago, in mentioning them you can show the recruiter a long track record of involvement.

You should add to that any personal awards or achievements that you might have received. If you've run a marathon or won a national tournament for Scrabble, let prospective employers know. These accomplishments signal that you have an inner determination, or that you like to compete. They also add to the picture of you as a human being and not just another name in the stack.

Sometimes, students will ask me if there's a place on the resume for their hobbies and interests. In my mind there definitely is. A resume, short as it is, should be like a one-on-one conversation. You want the person on the other end to feel like they're getting to know you, and one of the best ways to do that is to show them what you love and care about. Whether your passion is sports or stamp collecting doesn't matter. The fact that you're shedding a little light and coming across as a unique individual does. Besides, having activities outside of work makes you seem like a stronger and well-rounded candidate.

Of course, different qualities, achievements and activities all highlight different aspects of your character. Some might be more appropriate or beneficial for one job opening than another. With that in mind, you should probably have different versions of your resume. Most students know this, and go through the effort of printing out a copy with a new objective each time they apply for a job, but do little beyond that.

With all the time you've put into making yourself such a strong candidate, why stop there? See if you can do some background research and give yourself a leg up. For instance, you could find out from a contact in your target company what personality traits are important for the open job, and then tailor your resume to make sure you look like the exact person they need. Again, I'm not suggesting that you lie, stretch the truth, or try to be someone you aren't. Rather, I'm suggesting that if you know you've found a job that you're a great fit for, it only makes sense to put yourself in the best possible light. For example, if you know that travel will be a major part of your responsibilities, highlight your desire to see the world. Or, if you find out that the phone skills are a must, look for ways to make your interpersonal skills prominent. Tailoring your resume is about more than changing a couple of lines – it's about matching the parts of your personality that your new employer would need most.

To that end, you might even think about changing it based on which recruiter or hiring manager you're going to see. That might sound like taking things a bit far, but if you really want the job, then that's the kind of precision that's going to count. And if you don't want the job badly enough to take the extra time and effort, then you probably shouldn't be trying to get it anyway.

As you've probably gathered, there's a lot more to a warm resume than just a GPA or a list of talents and qualifications. If it's really going to do the job, it has to not only get you the interview, but also leave recruiters wanting to meet you. That takes an emotional connection. You want them to think, "This is somebody different. I wonder if they would seem half as great in person as they do on paper." When you begin your introduction with that kind of momentum, you can easily use it to carry over through the interview, to get the job.

Know the Risks

One of the toughest decisions for any job seeker is how much personal information to reveal on a resume. There are a lot of people, especially in light of the latest laws and regulations, who would advise you to make your resume as neutral as possible. In fact, human resources purists will even tell you that a recruiter shouldn't be able to tell anything about a person's gender, ethnicity, or age from their resume. From an ethical standpoint, they're absolutely right — all hiring should be blind. Employers should want to know that you're the right person for the job, and my experience has been that the overwhelming majority of them go into the recruitment process with exactly that mindset.

But, I always warn graduates that it is *possible* that someone will be biased — consciously or unconsciously — by the personal details you reveal on your resume. This is especially true with bigger issues like political affiliations, age, or religious views. It's not that all hiring managers are secretly bigots; it's that in the process of getting to know you, even on a sheet of paper, they're bound to form snap impressions — some of which may turn out to be true, and many of which probably won't.

Of course, the more generic you make your resume, the less likely it is to make an emotional connection with recruiters. So what should you do? Only you can decide that. I advise staying on the side of caution. If you've done campaigning for a Democratic candidate, for example, or are a member of the Young Republicans Club, I would simply list that you'd done "grass roots political work." Hiring managers love to know that you've been involved, and it removes the need to mention your affiliation. The same goes for anything that has to do with your religion. Saying that you've been active in your church or youth group is enough for most managers to know that you're outgoing and social, they don't want to know what faith or denomination you are.

Besides, even if you do decide to share personal details, some things are better left for an interview. For instance, recruiters and interviewers can't legally ask you whether or not you have children, and whether or not you decide to share that information is up to you. Bringing it up could make you seem like someone who will have trouble working long hours, or it could be something you use to show what a hard worker you are.

There are always going to be risks either way, so make decisions about which pieces of personal information to include on your resume carefully. Even though most recruiters won't be affected by them, there's really no need to take the risk.

Chapter 5

Your Cyber Persona

The explosion of information available on the Internet – especially about young people who have become accustomed to posting and seeing their personal details online – has added a new wrinkle to the job search process. There was a time, not too long ago, when if a prospective employer wanted to get a behind-the-scenes look at a job candidate, they had spring for an official background check. Those were expensive, took a lot of time, and usually only turned up basic data like whether somebody had any convictions, what their credit history was like, and if they'd ever used another name.

These days, though, finding out all about someone is as simple as turning on your computer. Major search engines like Google, Yahoo, and MSN crawl the Internet twenty four hours a day logging phrases and keywords for anyone who wants to find them. Since your name is one of those keywords, anybody with a dial up connection and a computer screen can learn personal details of your life.

Make no mistake; what's being written or shown about you on the Internet can cause serious damage to your job search. If there are incriminating photos, angry rants or other negative information floating around out there, it's going to come back to haunt you. Even the most technically-challenged recruiters know how to navigate to a search engine, and nobody's going to invest the kind of money that it takes to train a new team member without at least seeing what's been written about them online. What they find in those first few pages is going to form an impression that would be difficult to overcome – not that you're likely to get a chance. For all they know, your whole resume could be filled with lies, and lots of people turn out to be better interviewees than employees. If a quick online search shows that you might have problems fitting in or behaving professionally, it's going to be much too easy for them to just pass on you and not worry about it.

And so, the question that any student or graduate needs to ask themselves is this: *can my online persona survive a background check?*

The first step towards answering this is getting to know your online self. You need to find out what's out there before you give employers the chance to. Many young people are so used to working with their own websites, blogs, and social networking profiles that they have never taken the time to research themselves – much less from a prospective employer's point of view. Most are surprised at what they find, but the major problems can be summed up in one of two ways: either there's no information, or there's lots of it, and it's not good.

In the first case, the best thing to do is to start building an online profile now. Register for accounts with the major services like MySpace, Facebook, and LinkedIn. Not only can these sites serve as wonderful networking tools, but because they're so popular, search engine spiders (software programs that scour the Internet looking for new content and keywords for searchers) list them first. That means that whatever you add to your profile is going to show up on Google and other engines a lot faster and more prominently than it would on an obscure blog or webpage you start yourself.

If your problems run deeper, and there is negative information about you posted on the Internet, recognize that it's probably going to take some time to undo. The first step is to make a list of every item that you come across that might act as a red flag to prospective employers. In making that determination, be as cautious as possible. Assume that an employer is going to think the worst. This might sound harsh, but it's realistic. As we'll see in the next chapter, hiring people is an enormous financial risk – one that most new graduates can't even imagine. For that reason, recruiters can't afford to roll the dice; they don't want to bring you in if there's a chance you're going to be a problem. So, if they come upon photo after photo suggesting that you have a problem with drinking, or pictures of yourself in various states of undress, that's going to be a huge warning sign. Their best option at that point is to simply move on.

Luckily, removing negative information from the Internet isn't usually as hard as you might think. All you have to do, in most cases, is contact the owner or administrator of the website in question and ask them to remove the photo, article, or other material that could be harmful. Most companies don't want the hassle and bad press that would come with humiliating someone, especially a college student who's not in the public eye. Often, a simple e-mail will result in material being deleted immediately. This might not actually fix the problem right away, as many web pages are archived and backed up continuously, causing them to remain in search results for a while, but it's a good start. And if at first they don't respond, or if they refuse to remove the material, then simply be persistent. Usually, a few messages will get their attention.

When deciding which items to go after first, start with those that are the most damaging and prominent. For example, if a video of you committing a crime, or going topless on spring break appears on the first page of search results for your name, then focus your efforts there and don't move on until you've cleared them, because you're probably not getting a job until you have. Assuming there's nothing that harmful, your next step should be to ask for some help. See if you can get a few of your friends, professors, or professional contacts to search your name and see what they come up with. Because they might use different websites or keywords than you do, you could be surprised at what they come up with.

Next, go back through your own material. Examine all of the blogs, articles, and photos you've put online yourself. Many students are surprised at how much they've posted to the web and forgotten about. Now is the time to make sure that information isn't going to stop you from getting the job you want. Extend your search to your friends' websites and profiles as well. Lots of people like to post photos and details about the people they know. But with the tagging features on most sites, anything they've uploaded about you can be seen by everyone.

You might be thinking that this seems like a lot of work, and you'd be right. But is it worth it? I couldn't say for sure. Researching job candidates online has become standard practice, so it's not a question of whether you're going to be looked up online, but how deeply. A lot of the time, a one or two page search might do it. If your prospective employer doesn't find anything too upsetting, they might go ahead and call you in for an interview. A lot of bigger firms, though, are hiring background research companies these days. These go a lot farther, maybe even into your personal profiles and blogs. As with everything in the job search process, only you can decide what you're comfortable with. But it would be a shame to miss out on a great opportunity because some recruiter got the wrong impression from a stray photo, so if you ask me, it's better to just clean your online profile once and make sure it stays that way.

Get Proactive

While a lot of job seekers think about their online persona in terms of things that can keep them from getting hired, a better long-term approach is to generate a cyber profile that's stacked with positive information. In other words, why settle for having a recruiter come up with no negative information about you online, when you could create such a flood of helpful items that anyone who searches your name would be left with the impression that you are the greatest job candidate ever?

Like many of the tips in this book, this is a strategy that takes a while to use effectively. But done thoroughly, it can create such a landslide of momentum that virtually every interview you walk into will already be warmed.

The key to making it work is consistency. As I already mentioned, you should be sure to open up accounts with all the major social networking sites. Instead of posting info about parties, however, or what your favorite bands are, make sure that your pages and profiles reflect your professional ambitions. Write blog posts that talk about what's going on in the industry you want to work in, and take the time to upload photos of yourself with your professors, at association meetings, and so on. Make sure you keep everything positive, and don't go out of your way to brag. Remember, hiring managers want team players that are quietly confident. If you take the time to build your online profile, you won't have to blow your own horn because the Internet is going to do it for you.

If you want to go the extra mile, start doing some good things in the community. Most charities have their own websites and frequently post information about the volunteers and members who help them, along with pictures of their good deeds. What's more, they often forward them to the media, doubling the amount of good information about you online.

The net result is an Internet presence that's bragging about you twenty four hours a day. When a recruiter receives your resume, and decides to search your name, what they're going to find is page after page telling them about how professional you are, how involved you are in the field you're studying, all the great work you do for charity, and how grateful you are to your professors and advisors. Do you think they'd be excited to meet you, or that you've improved your chances of getting a job? Absolutely.

Your online persona is too important to leave to chance. Take the time to fill it with positive information, and it will soon become too outstanding for employers to ignore.

Chapter 6

Recruiter Reality

For all that's been said and written about recruiters – how to reach them, ways to mirror their body language, and so on – few students have a real understanding of who these men and women are, what they really want, and what goes through their minds when they look at resumes and interview graduates. In this chapter, I'm going to shed some light on that, because the only way to really get recruiters to notice you is to have a firm idea of what they're actually looking for and why.

One of the first things you should understand is that very few people you'll meet, especially when you're interviewing for an entry-level job, are going to be full-time recruiters. Most of the men and women sitting down across from you in the interview have other jobs and duties. In fact, meeting with new graduates like you probably represents a very small part of what they do. And so, as unlikely as it might seem, they're often as new to asking interview questions as you are to answering them.

And just like you, they have a certain level of anxiety about the process. Students sometimes have a hard time understanding this. After all, the person interviewing you already has the job. That's true, but deciding to hire someone is a very big decision. As you'll see in the section at the end of this chapter, their success or failure in finding the right person could end up costing their company an enormous amount of money. And so, even if they aren't the final decision maker, there's a lot of risk associated with recommending you for the next round. If you don't work out, your new company stands to lose big, and nobody wants to be responsible for destroying the bottom line.

If that weren't enough, recommending a new hire carries a good deal of professional risk. As I mentioned, most interviewers will pass you on to someone else if you make a good impression. Usually that person will be their manager. If your second interview isn't nearly as strong as your first, or worse, you come across as completely unprofessional or unprepared, that's going to reflect badly on the original interviewer. Their boss might end up wondering what they were thinking to recommend someone like that, or if the employee is a poor judge of character. Not only does that cause your interviewer to lose face, but it may even hurt their chances for a bonus or promotion down the line. After all, if they could recommend someone who's clearly a poor prospect to be hired, then what chance do they have at upper-level management?

Hopefully you're starting to understand the weight of the decision on your interviewer. As nervous as you feel about impressing them, they're just as worried about selecting the wrong person. This knowledge leads you to two key insights that most new graduates don't have. First, that most of the recruiters you meet are largely going to be risk averse. That is, they'd rather recommend a candidate who seems like a sure bet to fit into their team and company right away than they would someone who shows a lot of potential, but with some risks. And secondly, that what they love – the thing they're dying to have – is an easy choice.

Most new graduates go into the interview process with the wrong mindset. Anticipating tough questions and pressure-filled situations, they're convinced that an interviewer's mission is to screen out prospective employees until only one or two are left to be hired. In reality, though, recruiters don't want someone who has survived the process; they're looking for that one candidate who seems to stand head and shoulders above the rest. They want to meet a young man or woman who impresses them so much that they can easily and confidently recommend this person for further interviews and openings, without fear that the decision is going to come back and blow up in their face.

Keep these two concepts in mind as you begin your interviews. One of the first things a recruiter is going to try to find out is whether or not you seem to be the same kind of person that was advertised your resume. Every interviewer knows that job seekers have a tendency to stretch the truth, and even the ones who don't won't always live up to their qualifications. In other words, you may have all the credentials in the world, but if you come across as being an abrasive personality, are hard to work with, have a personal hygiene problem, or put up another warning sign, then you're not someone they want hanging around their company.

Figuring out whether or not you're "safe" is their number one priority. If you come up short in that regard, then there isn't anything left that will put you through to the next round of interviewers. This includes your skill set or technical background. As I hope I've impressed upon you by now, the attitude that you display in person is far more important than any initials or credentials on your resume. The right person, a team player with quiet confidence, can always be taught how to do the job, but a candidate with the wrong attitude is never going to fit in no matter what they know how to do.

Understanding this can also alleviate one of the bigger concerns that I frequently hear about – that you'll be discriminated against. Lots of students tell me that they worry they won't get the right job because of their ethnicity or gender, but the chance of this ever becoming an issue are incredibly small. I'm not going to tell you that the world is a perfect place, and that these things don't ever happen, but I can also say without hesitation that I've never witnessed it in any way, shape, or form. In more than twenty years, I haven't once seen a hiring manager who cared if he hired men or women, whites, blacks, or purples. For one thing, companies would never place a biased person in charge of evaluating candidates. Doing so wouldn't just open them up to lawsuits, but also rob them of some of the best young talent out there. On a deeper level, though, recruiters just want to find the right person; that concern trumps everything else.

So, having explained that interviewers aren't bigots, let me be quick to point out that they are still *people*. They have the same faults, issues, and shortcomings as the rest of us, and there may be times in the interview process where you'll have to overcome that. Again, I'm not talking about a situation where the recruiter is making a conscious effort to give you a hard time, but rather that they're distracted or preoccupied because of something outside your control.

Just as you had dozens or hundreds of other things going on in your life before the moment the interview began, so did the person on the other side of the desk. For all you know, you could have just met them on the best or worst day of their lives. They could have just found out that they're getting a bonus, or that their spouse is leaving them. They might have just learned that they're up for promotion, or that their department is going to be downsized. And these are just a few of the neatest examples. Your interviewer could be worried about their kids, vacation plans, or 1 million other things that are taking up their attention. Or, they could just be tired from working long hours meeting dozens of other job candidates.

This is especially true if you're meeting them on or near your college campus. I hate to say it, but drawing recruiting duty is often a "shortest straw" kind of deal. Everyone in the office is too busy as it is, so the least senior person gets chosen to travel, away from their work and families, to sit down and hear new graduates recite the same lines and answers to them for twelve hours a day. It's hard, in that situation, for them to stay focused and upbeat, especially when all the applicants seem so much alike.

My point is that you have to be prepared for every scenario. If your interviewer seems worn out or disengaged, the best thing you can do for yourself is to come across as energetic and enthusiastic. Be the breath of fresh air in the room. Don't count on the recruiter to provide the energy and enthusiasm. Often, by coming in with the right mindset, you can actually improve their mood. If you can accomplish that, you can create a strong impression that sets you apart from all the other young people they will meet in the first round of interviews.

The $250,000 Mistake

When I ask upcoming graduates how much they think an employer spends on hiring them, their answers tend to float around the amount of salary they expect to receive. When they offer this number, I tell them to think higher. Usually, after a moment or two, they'll think it through a bit and add in what they think the company spends on benefits, or maybe a bonus, but they're still well short of the real figure.

Believe it or not, the average bad hiring decision costs an employer *four to five times your annual salary*. So if they hire you for a $50,000 year job, for instance, and you don't work out, they've just lost a quarter of a million dollars. To understand how this can be, you need to look at the situation from a much wider perspective than most students are used to.

For example, your salary wasn't the first expense. In order to select you, they had to pay a recruiter to sift through potential resumes and then sit down with each candidate. They might have used an outside firm for this, or simply paid overtime or other expenses to employees who are on staff. The true cost of those working hours alone could run into the thousands, and you can add to that the travel expenses that were incurred, along with the manager's time when they did the longer follow-up interviews. And of course, if they ran a background check for a drug test, those costs need to be figured in.

Then, there's all the money they spend once you're hired. This includes your salary, of course, but also the travel and training that was required to get you up to speed – both of which can be costly. Furthermore, they probably paid you for a least a few months while you figured out how to do your job. That means a chunk of salary and benefits going to a staff member who probably isn't producing all that much.

Once it's clear that you're not a good fit for the job, these costs are compounded, because they either have to go through expense legally preparing to let you go, or keep paying you while you underperform. As that happens, you're liable to bring down the morale of the department and under serve the company's clients and customers, which can result in lost business or other employees leaving. The real costs of those consequences could easily stretch into the millions.

I could go on and on, but I hope you're beginning to understand why hiring a person, even for an entry-level job, represents an enormous risk to any company. So, when you next meet with a recruiter, ask yourself the question that's probably in their mind: have I made it clear to them that I'm worth a $250,000 gamble?

Then, there's all the money they spend once you're hired. This includes your salary, of course, but also the travel and training that was required to get you up to speed – both of which can be costly. Furthermore, they probably paid you for a least a few months while you figured out how to do your job. That means a chunk of salary and benefits going to a staff member who probably isn't producing all that much.

Once it's clear that you're not a good fit for the job, these costs are compounded, because they either have to go through expense legally preparing to let you go, or keep paying you while you underperform. As that happens, you're liable to bring down the morale of the department and under serve the company's clients and customers, which can result in lost business or other employees leaving. The real costs of those consequences could easily stretch into the millions.

I could go on and on, but I hope you're beginning to understand why hiring a person, even for an entry-level job, represents an enormous risk to any company. So, when you next meet with a recruiter, ask yourself the question that's probably in their mind: have I made it clear to them that I'm worth a $250,000 gamble?

Chapter 7

Interview Preparation

Even if you've followed every piece of advice in this book as closely and perfectly as humanly possible, the interview is still going to be the make or break moment in your job search. For that reason, I'm going to spend this chapter and the next two getting you ready. As you read them, keep in mind everything I've said so far. Interviewing might be a big topic, and it might seem a bit overwhelming at first, but when it's all said and done the whole process is designed to help find out whether you're the right person for the opening. If you can convey that to recruiters every step of the way, then you're going to be offered the job.

Besides, becoming a world-class interviewee isn't really as hard as it looks. All it really takes to separate yourself from every other candidate out there is *practice* and *preparation*. We're going to talk about both of these now.

To get comfortable interviewing, you have to do same thing you do to get comfortable with anything else:

practice. That's why, for my money, the very best way to prepare for an interview is going through dozens of mock interviews. These are just what they sound like – pretend interviews where you have friends or professional contacts try to evaluate you the way a prospective employer would. I conduct these with students all the time, and it's amazing to see how much their confidence can grow in just a few sessions.

They can also lend a lot of insight about where you are in terms of your preparation. I sat one young man down for a mock interview a few years ago, and started in with what I thought were some relatively normal questions. He started to get a bit flustered, but we pushed through so that he could get some valuable experience. About halfway in, however, he actually broke down in tears. It suddenly dawned on him how unprepared he was to look for a job in the real world.

Believe it or not, this was actually a good thing. Painful as it might have been, that experience led him to undergo dozens more mock interviews, until he eventually grew very comfortable with the process. Once he got past his anxiety, and began to understand the nature of the questions being asked (something we'll talk about in the next chapter) he discovered that they weren't so intimidating after all.

There are actually two lessons in that story. The first is the same point I've been trying to make: that you should practice your interviewing skills early and often.

The second, though, relates to who you should practice with. Your mock interviews should be conducted with someone who's been in the working world for at least a few years. You don't want your roommate or best friend interviewing you for the same reason that you wouldn't want your grandmother teaching you how to hit a fastball – they're going to take it too easy on you. Part of the game is learning to anticipate and deal with tough, unexpected questions, because that's what's going to build up that quiet confidence you'll need to show when you meet with real recruiters.

For this reason, professors and mentors can be great mock interviewers if they have the time and inclination to help you out. But if you really want to do things the right way, why not turn to the professionals? The men and women at your career services center have probably given thousands of mock interviews. They don't just know how to push you, but also how to critique your performance. Instead of telling you that you did well and you should practice, they can point you in precisely the areas you need to work on, so don't overlook them as your mock interview resource.

Along the same lines, one practice that I see taught and recommended in a number of places, and one that I fiercely disagree with, is going on practice interviews. That is, applying to real jobs with actual companies even though you have no desire or intention of working for them. I understand the appeal; getting out there and going a few rounds with a lot of recruiters seems like an easy way to get comfortable with the process. However, I still think it's a big mistake, and there are two reasons why.

First, there's the fact that you're being dishonest. I know from experience that recruiters are busy people who have a hard enough time fitting all their work into the available days and hours. The last thing they need is to see another face without the possibility of filling their open position. You wouldn't want to work for free or have somebody waste your time, so you shouldn't ask anyone else to, either.

A better reason, though, is that it can create a false confidence. When students go on practice interviews, it's similar to taking batting practice. Sure, you can work on your swing, but it's not the same as a live game setting would be. Most recruiters will notice very quickly if you're just going through the motions, and so they won't ask you the tough questions they would put to a real candidate – assuming they don't just terminate the interview out right. And even if they do, you're not going to learn a great deal from the process because you're not emotionally invested. You don't want the job anyway, so there's no incentive for you to push yourself. If anything, you're probably going to come up with some bad habits.

Practicing, in the form of mock interviews, definitely gives you a leg up when it comes to preparing for the real thing.

But don't waste a recruiter's time, or your own, by showing up to interview for a job you don't want.

Once you've familiarized yourself with interviews in general, you'll want to get yourself ready for the specific meetings you have coming up. The way to do that is by arming yourself with as much information as possible. Hopefully, you've got a great idea of what kind of job you're looking for in the kinds of companies that can hire you to do it. It's even better if you've built your network, gotten involved in some industry associations, and come to know a few people who are working in the field, because that's going to make the in-depth preparation a lot easier than it will be otherwise.

Start by learning about your prospective employer. You can begin with general company guides, like those you'd find on Hoover's or any other major business website. In them, you'll find information about the company, earnings, who the top executives are, and so on. You don't have to memorize any of these facts; just try to form a general picture of what they're doing, how they're making money, and where they are positioned in the marketplace.

After that, see if you can find out about the job in question. Who held it before? What happened to them? Or if it's a new job, why is the company adding it? If at all possible, speak to someone who's had the job, or at least worked with the person who did. Find out what the best qualities for a candidate are, or what they wish the former employee had done differently or better.

One secret weapon I learned from a mentor of mine long ago, and that I've shared with seminar attendees over the years, is to familiarize yourself with your prospective employer's revenue stream. Find out how money comes into the company, where they make their profits, and how the job you would be taking fits into that picture. By getting to know these details ahead of time, you make yourself ready to speak directly to the recruiter's hiring concerns. After all, whomever they bring in is going to have to bring more money to the business than they cost – directly or indirectly – so if you can show them how you'll add to sales, increase efficiency, or decrease expenses, then you're well ahead of the game. What's more, when you take this kind of inside information to an interview, the recruiter will be stunned. That's because most candidates, especially those just leaving school, aren't nearly savvy enough to think of these kinds of things.

And speaking of the recruiter, find out whatever you can about who will be interviewing you, along with their position, background, and other details. Look at them the same way they would be examining you as a job candidate. Start with the Google search, and then move on to mutual acquaintances or other resources if they're available. You're trying to find two things here: one is a sense of their personality. The more you know about their demeanor, the better you can prepare for the style and tone of their questions. Secondly, you're looking for commonalities. People always like to know and work with other people who are most like themselves. By finding out that you went to the same school, share the same fraternity, or have a common interest in something, you can create a feeling of familiarity that will leave a strong impression in an interviewer's mind.

No matter how much groundwork you do, you're still going to have to get through at least a couple of interviews to get the job you want. But if you can take the time to practice and prepare, you'll have an easy time doing it, because you've been there before and know what to expect.

Creating a Braggable Binder

If you really want an unfair advantage in your interview preparation, then I recommend you put together what I call a "Braggable Binder." This is a simple technique, and one that goes by lots of different names, but few students I talk to have ever used it, or even heard of it.

To get started, you'll only need an everyday notebook binder, a few clear plastic inserts, and a couple of hours. The idea is to brainstorm all of your great qualities and achievements. Try to come up with every award, recognition, and accolade you can think of. As you do this, take the time to really dig deeply. Don't just include the first few things that come into your head. In fact, it's not a bad idea to ask your friends and relatives if they can think of anything you might have forgotten.

Once you're sure you've come up with everything that might be impressive to a prospective employer, start digging up the evidence on as many of them as you can and putting them into the binder, in order of the most impressive to the least. If what you have is easy to file, like award certificates or thank you letters, include them as they are. If, on the other hand, you come across items like trophies or medals that won't fit in the binder, then take a picture and place that inside. The end result should be a series of pages that would show any recruiter what a fantastic candidate and human being you are.

This is the point where a lot of students stop me. "This sounds like a great idea," they say, "but I'm not going to pull out a list of my awards in front of the recruiter." Not to worry, I don't expect you to. Instead, you're going to use the oldest sales trick in the book – bringing an item to a meeting and not mentioning it. Sooner or later, assuming the interview is going well, the recruiter is going to ask you what's in the notebook. At that point, you can simply mention that you brought a few letters of reference and some other materials "just in case you wanted to see them." They will, and at that point, you've just gotten the interviewer to ask to see your portfolio success – something probably no other graduate has done.

And even if you don't get to that point, it's still well worth it to put your Braggable Binder together. That's because the real value is in the time you spend assembling it. By looking for awards, certificates, and other reminders of your accomplishments, you're forcing yourself to remember all of the great things you've done throughout your high school and college career. This not only helps your confidence and self esteem throughout the process, but also makes them fresher and easier to talk to prospective employers about. It's hard to forget your best qualities and achievements when you've just spent a few hours looking them over.

The Braggable Binder is a simple tactic, but one that can put your interview preparation over the edge. Don't miss the chance to show employers – and yourself – what a great candidate you are.

Chapter 8

You're Up

So, after years of school and weeks or months of intense preparation, you're finally ready to go out and take a crack at getting your first real job. I congratulate you. You've worked hard to get to this point, and if you can keep your head on straight throughout the rest of the process, it's about to start paying off for you. In this chapter I'm going to show you what to look out for in the first half of your interview.

First, realize that the interview begins the moment you're within eyesight of anyone who works for your prospective employer. This includes the greeting you give the receptionist, and the time spent waiting in the office. You're *always* being evaluated. More likely than not, your interviewer is going to ask other people who met you what their impressions were, so act like a professional and make them count.

In fact, one popular tactic these days is to invite all the candidates for a job, either before the first or second round of interviews, to a dinner reception beforehand. Sharp candidates realize that this is a form of interviewing, but most don't really know what the recruiter is actually looking for. While a lot of graduates suspect that it's whether they use the right fork, or the cleanliness of their cars, the truth is that most hiring managers just want to see how you carry yourself. Do you seem to know how to behave professionally? Are you the kind of person they would feel comfortable having in their office, or sending on a business trip? Whether you first meet your new employer at an office, a restaurant, or a job fair, put your best self forward, and follow the same guidelines I'm about to give you just like you would if you were sitting across the desk from a recruiter.

I mentioned in the beginning of this book that I wasn't going to talk in any great detail about the basics, because I assume you already know them. That rule still stands here, except to mention how incredibly important it is that you make a good first impression with your appearance, handshake, and greeting. In the thousands of interviews I've done, the candidate has set the tone nearly every time within the first five or ten seconds. If they come in with an aura of calm and confidence, that will almost always last for the time we're together. But, if I get the distinct impression that they are uncomfortable – or even unlikable – then it's very unlikely they'll make it through to the next round. The lesson here is that, once again, the basics really do matter. Make sure your appearance and first impressions are strong.

As a side note to that, one question that I'm hearing more and more these days is whether a new graduate should cover up their tattoos or piercings for an interview. I suppose the best answer is "it depends." While there would undoubtedly be some recruiters who would be turned off by these, I personally think they can be great personal expressions. Plus, they can sometimes lead you to tell the interviewer a great story about how you came to get them — especially if it shows teamwork or devotion to a cause. And finally, I'm a big believer in letting people know who you are. Think of it this way: if you've got a large tattoo or piercing that you're especially proud of, how happy are you going to be working for someone who doesn't approve of it? I can't tell you whether you should show off your jewelry or body art in an interview, just realize that it's not a cut and dried decision either way.

Once you've gotten your greetings out of the way, your interviewer will probably make a few minutes of small talk. They might ask a couple of soft questions about where you're from, or how you're enjoying your last few weeks of college life, but they're not too concerned with the answers. They just want to put you at ease and get a taste of your personality. That's not to say that you shouldn't be thinking about the answers you give; as you'll see in the section at the end of this chapter, a candidate who isn't careful can hurt their chances in the first few minutes by not thinking things through. For the most part, though, you'll just want to come across as open and relaxed.

Assuming you haven't done anything tragic up to this point, you'll be ready for the "real" interview to begin. The recruiter will start to ask you questions about your credentials, background, and attitude to see if you're a good fit for the job opening. This is where most traditional interview books focus their attention, and with good reason – the answers you give will determine your future with the company.

For that reason, and because so many young people get tripped up on the same handful of questions, I've included the five biggest show-stoppers you need to look out for, along with the best ways to handle them. While all interview questions are important, and I really do encourage you to spend some time going over the basics, these are the ones that will separate the best candidates from the pack.

Why Should We Hire You?

Interviewers love this question because it cuts right to the heart of the matter. After all, the reason they've set aside an hour or more of their day is to find out whether or not you are the best person for their open position. What better way to find out than by seeing how you handle being asked directly?

Unfortunately, many new graduates misinterpret it, thinking that the interviewer wants to know about their business or industry skills. Certainly, that's part of it; no company wants to hire someone who has no idea how to use a telephone or computer. But, as we've seen, the fact that you've graduated from college, and that they've already had a look at your resume, indicate that they already think you have the basic skills you'll need to learn the job.

With that in mind, when interviewers ask why they should hire you, realize that what they're looking for goes beyond how fast you can type or which computer classes you completed. They're trying to uncover that sense of quiet confidence that I keep coming back to. They want someone who isn't going to be a prima donna, but someone who is going to pitch in right away without whining or complaining about what is or isn't "their job." So, when the question of why the interviewer should hire you is asked, make sure you come across as being competent. But more importantly, show that you have a willingness to get involved and do what you can to help your new department or company.

What Are Your Weaknesses?

This is the classic interview trip-up question. And, if the thousands of new graduates I've spoken to are any guide, it's also one of the most hated. By asking about your weaknesses, interviewers are basically inviting you to give a few reasons why you shouldn't be hired... aren't they?

Actually, believe it or not, they aren't. The big pitfall here isn't in revealing a part of yourself that's less than perfect — it's in avoiding the question altogether. Most people, when asked about their weaknesses in an interview, will give one of a handful of stock answers: *I work too hard*, *I take my work home with me*, *I'm too driven*, and so on. They think they're highlighting what a great candidate they are, but what they're really doing is failing to set themselves apart from the competition. What's more, they're showing that they're not comfortable enough in their own skin to admit to areas where they can improve.

The best way to answer this question, as surprising as it might be, is to be *honest*. No one's expecting you to blurt out that you're an addict or embezzler, but go ahead and be up front about one of your faults. For example, you might admit that you hate criticism, or that you have a habit of being too direct with other people. Don't stop there, though. Once you've been open about your weakness, tell the interviewer what you're doing to improve it. Demonstrate that you're open enough to tell the truth, and that you're constantly working to become a better employee and person.

When you take this approach, two great things happen. First, you don't come across like just another programmed interviewee who will say just about anything to get the job. And second, you get the chance to make a personal connection with the human being on the other side of the desk. All of us, even your interviewer, have aspects of our personalities that we'd like to change. By sharing one of your challenges, you make it easier for them to see you as a person – one they might like, and even hire.

How Would Other People Describe You?

This is another question where the urge to give stock answers can really hurt your chances for another interview. Lots of people like to say that they are funny, outgoing, helpful, etc. *So what?* You just described 90% of the population, not to mention the other dozen people interviewing for the job.

So think long and hard about how you're going to answer this question when it comes up in the interview. You don't have to say anything crazy or outlandish, but you do want to find a thought or phrase that sets you apart from everyone else. For that reason, *risk-taking, entrepreneurial,* or *precise* are all better answers than happy, fun, or hard-working. They highlight your best qualities, but do so in a way that isn't completely generic.

Whatever you come up with, though, make sure that it actually does describe you. Your interviewer is looking to see whether the answers you give are consistent with the other pieces of information they have to work with, including your resume, appearance, body language, and answers to other questions. If it seems like you're offering a description of yourself — even an interesting one — that doesn't match up with everything else they've seen, they may be left with doubts about your honesty and sincerity.

If you're not sure what words would best describe you, take the time before your interview to ask your friends, family members, or professors what words or phrases they would use. Keep a couple of the best answers, and you get an easy way to deal with one of the toughest interview questions.

What Would You Do in This Situation...?

Every interviewer knows that they're probably seeing you on your best day. With your suit pressed, your hair freshly cut, and a crisp resume tucked in your briefcase, you are more prepared than ever to show off your good qualities. But their job isn't to evaluate you on your best day; it's to see how you'll perform in the real world. One of the easiest ways for them to do that, even if it's just hypothetical, is to put you in a different situation. And so, they'll ask you "what would you do *if*..."

There are endless variations on this question: some interviewers will ask whether you like to be a wallflower or the life of the party, others will want to know what you would do if you saw your coworker or boss stealing from the company, and still another twist is seeing how you, a prospective employee, would handle a miscommunication or major business mistake. No matter what form it takes, though, this question's aim is always the same – to get under the glossy exterior and see what the candidate has under the hood.

Keep that in mind as you field these questions. The actual setting or situation isn't all that important. What the interviewer really wants to know is how you handle stress, what your personal ethics are like, or whether you are easily frustrated. In other words, the question isn't that important, but how you handle it *is*.

The first thing to do is stay calm. Resist the urge to jump in right away and speak. Instead, think for a moment about what is being asked and what the interviewer really wants to know. If they are trying to get at your interpersonal skills, then speak to that. On the other hand, if they're trying to find out about your honesty level, put that at the forefront of your answer. Then, try to bring your response around to an actual experience in your own life. Rather than saying what a great employee you'd be, let them see how you've handled yourself in the past.

Questions about hypothetical situations are hard, but if you can use them to talk about times when you dealt with real-world challenges, you'll come through with flying colors.

What Do You Love?

This is my favorite interview question, and it's one that I think you should answer, whether you get it or not. Let me explain: the number one thing that recruiters want see out of any job candidate is attitude and passion. I want to feel like they've made the effort to connect with me as an actual person, and that I'm getting a glimpse of their true self – what they love and admire in this world – rather than a carefully constructed picture that they've put together to get the job. By asking, "What do you love?" I can pull away at all of those layers, and invite them to tell me about what matters most to them.

Ironically enough, I don't really care what the answer is, so long as it's genuine. I've had lots of people tell me that they love their family, or that they are involved in some kind of charitable organization, but I'm just as happy to hear that they enjoy collecting bottle caps. Either way, they've shown me that they've got something deeper to them than what I get from their GPA or letters of recommendation. I've gotten a peek at what they're really made of, and it makes it that much easier for me to want them on my team.

That's why I say you should answer this question whether you get it or not. A lot of interviewers aren't going to come right out and ask you what your personal passions are, but that doesn't mean you can't bring it up in your other answers, or highlight specific achievements that you're proud of on your resume. I'm not saying that you should derail an explanation of your technical expertise by talking about how much you love deep-sea fishing; what I *am* saying, though, is that you should take the opportunity to present yourself as a whole person — not just a candidate for a job, but someone who cares about more than a paycheck.

If you can comfortably handle these questions, then you should be just fine with anything else the interviewer throws at you. That's because, even though the individual responses might be different, the themes to your answer should all be the same — that you're a positive up-and-coming professional. Every piece of information you share should just add to that picture and make you seem upbeat and bright, rather than bitter and unsteady.

Remember, too, the tough questions are actually a great sign. For one thing, they mean that the interviewer is taking an interest in you. They wouldn't bother putting you under any pressure if they weren't considering you for their position. And at the same time, every graduate can answer the easy ones; the challenging questions uncover real character. They're the places where most candidates are going to be unprepared and fail, so by handling them smoothly, you can easily set yourself apart from everyone else that the interviewer has seen.

Don't Make Unforced Errors

In the sports world, the term "unforced error" refers to a mistake made by a player for what seems to be no good reason. These are the dropped fly balls, missed open baskets, and open field fumbles that drive coaches and fans so crazy. I also think they're a good analogy to one of the most common interview mistakes.

The fact that you're always being evaluated in an interview setting should be clear. As a candidate, however, you should realize that this extends to *every* part of the interview — even the parts that seem informal.

After your greeting and introductions, your interviewer will most likely get started by asking you a few easy questions. They might even be as simple as "how is your day?" or "how is your job search going so far?" Because these are such laid back inquiries, some graduates are tempted to respond with long, rambling answers, or worse, by saying something negative. It might not seem like a big deal to mention how tired you are, or that you just wish you could get a job already, but doing so changes the entire impression a recruiter has of you. Remember, your job is to appear positive, upbeat, and professional. If you're coming across as angry or sullen within a few minutes of meeting them, what conclusion are they likely to draw?

Naturally, there's a fine line here. As I hope you realize by now, one of your toughest challenges is to come across like an actual person, rather than a talking resume. It's okay to show a little bit of personality when a recruiter asks you to talk about yourself, or give your opinion on a topic. The point, though, is to think of that image you're trying to put forward, and make sure that your answers are consistent with that.

Most unforced interview errors take place in the first few minutes when the new graduate has their guard down, but try to maintain your focus and discipline throughout your time with the recruiter. There's never a good time to create a negative impression of yourself or your attitude, but there's always a chance to keep building your case as the best person for the job.

Chapter 9

Turning the Tables

Many new graduates, understandably, focus their interview preparation on the kinds of questions they expect to get and the answers they plan to give to them. I can understand this call; that's likely to be the toughest and longest part of the interview process, and you're going to have to do well to have any chance of getting hired. Be aware, though, that when the interviewer has heard everything they need, they're going to put the ball in your court. And when they do, it's your chance to seal the deal.

Usually, this will happen in a very straightforward way. After half an hour or forty minutes, the recruiter is going to ask if you have any questions for them. You should. The inquiries you put to them are especially beneficial, because they allow you to find out more information about the job and company, but also because asking the right ones can set you apart from other candidates. Surprisingly, however, many graduates fail to take advantage. They either ask about one or two procedural issues, or say they don't have any questions at all. This can create doubt in the interviewer's mind. After all, if you don't have anything you want to ask about the position, the company, or the process, how interested could you really be in getting the job? You've come too far in the process to let the interview slip away, so I'm going to give you the most powerful questions to close your meeting with, and why.

"Why has this position opened up?"

This is a great question - almost any answer to it helps you to get a better understanding of the job. For example, if the interviewer responds that the last employee was promoted, then you can know for certain that there are advancement opportunities available. Likewise, if they mention that they've had a hard time finding the right person to hold it down long-term, that could be a clue that the stress, pain, or some other part of the job is keeping others away. It doesn't necessarily mean you don't want the position, but it gives you an opening to ask your interviewer why more people don't see it as a long-term option.

For most entry-level jobs, you'll likely that find promotions and lateral moves are common as new graduates get familiar with the company and go on to roles with more responsibilities, or that the job is a new one within the company. Neither of those tell you a great deal, but they still help you know what you should expect if you're hired, as well as what the company would expect of you.

"What opportunities for advancement are there in this position?"

This is one every well-prepared graduate should ask. Inquire about the potential for growth and you kill two birds with one stone. First, you find out if the job leads anywhere, and how quickly. If a common path is from that position to management, for example, then you can start to form an idea of where you'd move on to, how quickly, and what sort of pay and incentive packages would be involved. Secondly, you make it clear to the interviewer that you have plans for your future. No ambitious young professional – and especially the kind you been working to become if you've followed the advice in this book – is going to accept a position that doesn't offer the potential for advancement. This is a backhanded way of letting the recruiter know that you're planning on going places, and that's a quality they love in new graduates.

"How did you get started working for this company?"

The real value in this question is in establishing an emotional connection with your interviewer. Every single person on the planet is their own favorite topic of conversation, and by inviting them to open up and tell their story, you make the interview conversation more two-sided. Allowing the interviewer to tell you about their background also brings out some of their personality, which makes it easier for them to like and trust you. And, you might even find out that they used to have your job, and can give you some insight into what it's like and how to get started. In the end, though, they may or may not tell you anything useful about the company or the position you'd be taking. That's okay; you just want them to open up a little, because that's going to make it much easier for them to hire you.

"How would what's going on in the industry right now affect the position?"

There are number of different ways you could ask something like this, but what you want to do is let the interviewer know that you've done your homework and are aware of the major trends going on in their company and industry. You might ask something specifically about a new technology, their management structure, a new product, or something else altogether. But no matter what it is, it's a good idea to ask a specific question if you can, because the recruiter has probably just sat through a dozen or more interviews where the other person knew little about the company beyond the fact that they had a job opening. By coming across as engaged and informed, you make yourself easy to hire.

"What will be the next step in the interview process?"

This is a good question because it can help you set realistic expectations for the remainder of the interview process. If your interviewer answers, for instance, that they'll be seeing dozens of candidates and that you should expect to hear from someone in human resources within the next 2 to 3 weeks, then you know you're going to be in for a long ride at best. On the other hand, if they tell you that you'll be speaking to Mr. or Mrs. so-and-so next week, then you can proceed more confidently. After all, they've just told you that you've done well enough to earn another interview, and what the timeframe for that looks like.

A good strategy in that case, and in fact with all of these questions, is to ask follow-ups. If you're told that your next interview will be with someone else in the company, for example, take the chance to ask a little about that person. Use the time you have to find out a few facts or details that will help you prepare for the next step. Or, find out a little more about what qualities are important for the open position, so that you can practice emphasizing those in your mock interviews. The point is to use the time you have efficiently. Sitting across from you is someone who could tell you just about everything you need to know about the job and the hiring process, so try to walk away as prepared as possible.

That being said, exercise common sense. If the interviewer has already given you an hour of their time, ask a few of your most important questions and then let them get back to their day. There's a fine line between coming across as ambitious and becoming a burden to your interviewer. I would say that you shouldn't ask more than a half-dozen questions, and try to be aware of their body language and the tension level. If it looks like they need to get rid of you, excuse yourself before they have to. Besides, you should be grabbing one of their business cards for follow up anyway. Besides sending thank you letters, there's nothing wrong with using these to ask a question or two over the phone at a convenient time.

It's a good idea to write out your biggest questions before the interview and add to it as needed. It's easy, after the mentally grueling process of describing yourself to another person for the better part of an hour, to lose track of what you meant to find out by the time it's over. Besides, having some written questions in hand makes you seem more focused and organized.

When you've reached the end of an interview, it can be tempting to shake hands, breathe a sigh of relief, and head home to wait for the recruiter's next call. But by asking a few questions of your own, you come across as someone who knows what they're doing – and the kind of candidate who's sharp enough to make an immediate impact on the company.

Making the Interview Easy

I'm going to share with you something that I almost feel guilty about revealing, so I ask you to please use it responsibly and promise not to tell anyone you heard it from me.

If you will remember from a few chapters back, I told you that one of the things that most students didn't realize was that recruiters are usually filling a part-time role. They're not professional interviewers, and so they're just following a basic script of questions to get to know you. Because of that, you can use a series of follow-up and redirected questions to continually turn the tables during an interview and sidestep a lot of the tougher questions they might normally ask. I'll caution you from the start that this is definitely an advanced technique, and one that won't work on veteran recruiters. Still, if you can pull it off, it's a great method to try.

It goes like this: instead of waiting for the interviewer to ask if you have any questions, you simply follow one of your answers with a question directed at them. For example, suppose your interviewer asks where you see yourself in five years. You give them your answer, by the end, you add on" how did you come to be in your position?" Because they aren't skilled interviewers, and they enjoy talking about themselves, many recruiters will spend several minutes or longer telling you the story of their career. Sometimes, this can yield valuable insights into the way the company works. Other times, it's just a good way of building rapport with the person who's interviewing. After all, the more time they spend talking about their lives, the happier they are going to be and the more they're going to like you.

Obviously, you'll have to answer some questions and give up some details to leave a strong enough impression to be considered for the next round. But another way to open up your interviewer is by continually bringing the conversation back around to things you have in common. For instance, imagine that a recruiter asks you to talk about your biggest weaknesses. Maybe you admit to not being as patient as you'd like, but then mention how you've taken up chess or painting to improve your patience and concentration. And then, you add on "because I think those will be important qualities for my career, don't you agree?" Just like before, you're inviting the recruiter to participate in the discussion and offer his or her opinion. They may only give you a yes or no, but they also might take the bait and tell you about areas where they're trying to improve, or personality traits that the two of you have in common. And again, you're building that two-way bridge of communication, and making the interview seem like a friendly conversation instead of a tense business interaction.

Opening up your interviewer and getting them to talk is a great way to build rapport, and also to take some of the pressure out of the room. It won't work all the time, but if you practice it enough, you'll be pleasantly surprised at what it can do for you.

Chapter 10

On the Job

Since this book is about getting the job you want, not working at it, I realize that a lot of you might decide to skip over this chapter. Still, after all the work I've ask you to put in up to this point, I feel it's only fair that I give you some tips and advice for turning your first real job into a jumping off point for the rest of your career.

But first things first. At some point, whether it's in an interviewer's office or over the phone, you're going to be offered the job. Even if you can barely keep yourself from jumping up and down and screaming with joy, do the professional thing and tell the recruiter you'd like to consider the offer for a day or two. Doing so allows you to seem more in control of the process, and it also gives you a little bit of time to do some last minute reflection and decide whether this is the right opportunity for you. Employers expect this, so no one is going to be put off by your not accepting on the spot.

Some books and experts would advise you to try to negotiate your starting salary, bonuses, or other factors. Frankly, unless you've got a lot of offers or really, really unusual talent or skill set, I don't recommend this. That's because most entry-level jobs have a very tightly controlled pay range. The company knows what you are worth and what they should expect to pay, so you aren't likely to get too much more than that listed on your offer letter. I think that your energy is better spent learning everything you can and planning ahead for your first promotion — when you might have more control over the salary and benefits.

Once you're actually working at your new company, the best rule of thumb I can give you — regardless of the job or industry — is to be indispensable. That is, try to become the one person in the office that people turn to for help, advice, and opinions. Be the glue that holds everything together. Employers love young people who come in with that attitude, because they often end up as high-level managers. Become the one person your boss knows they can count on, and you'll always be appreciated.

Along the same lines, never take your job for granted. One of the things that I've told new graduates for years is to treat their position as if they were on an independent contracting gig that could go away tomorrow. In other words, imagine that you were your own one-person company. What would you be able to offer your employer? How would you justify the cost? Anytime you don't have the answers to those questions, you're losing sight of the reasons that your employer has to keep you around. Remember, at some point they're in business to make money. If you're not helping them reach that objective, directly or indirectly, then it's only a matter of time before they decide your salary is an unnecessary expense.

Another good piece of advice is to never stop learning. There are a lot of people, sadly enough, who finish school and never crack another book open again. As a consequence, the rest of the world − not to mention their industry − passes them by. In order to stay fresh and up to date, you're going to have to take a look through a few professional magazines once in a while, or flip through a title on management, efficiency, sales, or some other part of your job. In fact, if you can make this a regular habit, as I do, you can build a massive competitive advantage over your peers. That's because, in time, you'll know a lot more about your business than they do. Managers will notice this, and you'll start to rise to the top.

Try to surround yourself with positive people. If there's one thing that will make or break your career, it's going to be the company you keep. Psychologists have shown time and again that we tend to adopt the attitudes and beliefs that we're surrounded by most often. So, if you make a point of hanging out with other people who are on their way to fantastic careers, then the odds are you will, too. But if you spend all of your time with slackers and complainers, you're going to find that you run out of energy and motivation pretty quickly.

And don't just think about the people who are immediately around you at work, either. Remember that network you put together during your years on campus? Try to keep up to speed with those folks. As you get busier in your job, and maybe even move around the country, you're not going to see your contacts as often as you might like. Still, make sure that they are receiving cards and e-mails from you from time to time. For one thing, it's just good business to know as many people as you can. You never know when someone on your list will need a product or service your company provides, or vice versa. And in a more concrete sense, maintaining a network is a good hedge against the future. It's a sad fact that today's global economy has made job security a thing of the past. No matter how well you do in your career, and how high you climb, there's always the possibility that what's here today will be gone tomorrow. But if you make a point of improving yourself professionally a little at a time, and keeping up with your contacts, there's always going to be a place for you at a great company.

In fact, I would advise you to always make the point of glancing at the horizon now and again. Even if nothing happens to your job, and if your company keeps plugging along as always, there's a very good chance that you'll decide you're ready for a change at some point. Sometimes people just need new challenges, and the trend in recent decades has been towards more jobs and careers, not fewer. You may find that you're happy just where you are, but if you're not, then don't be afraid to try new options and avenues.

My degree was in marketing, and I spent my college years envisioning case studies, focus groups, and other campaign-centered tasks. Since then, however, I've been in sales, management, and professional speaking. Did I draw up that way? No. Would I change a thing if I could? Absolutely not. Life has a funny way of taking you where you need to go, not where you plan on ending up. Keep following your passions, and putting yourself in a position to succeed, and you'll never have to worry too much about where your career is going.

Generations at Work

A lot of new graduates, without the benefit of experience in the working world, are surprised to find just how diverse today's business world really is. What they find is that most people, by virtue of age, experience, or background, aren't going to see the world in the same way they do.

When I first began researching the employment process, one of the most fascinating things that I came across was the different points of view that people tend to hold based on what generation they're from. For example, baby boomers tend to be very goal and work oriented. A lot of these folks are in their late 50s and early 60s now, putting them at the heads of many companies and departments. They like signs of achievement and recognition, and are motivated to earn those by results. That's why many of those values are reflected in major corporations today.

When my generation, Generation X, came along we brought a different sense of where we saw our careers taking us. Not only did we place a much bigger priority on technology than our parents did, but we were known as being more individualistic, and striving for a work/life balance over material achievements.

And to this day, we're generally thought of as being a little more flexible and free flowing than our more experienced peers.

Today's new employees – the generation Y graduates I meet every week – are putting their own spin on things, too. Only time will tell how you evolve, but so far you seem to draw out some of the best qualities of those who came before you. For example, you're certainly more tech savvy than my generation ever was, and just as concerned about your social and family lives, but while maintaining a sense of that goal-oriented focus that the baby boomers were known for.

One of the challenges that you're likely to face as you begin your career is fostering and maintaining your relationships with managers and coworkers outside of your own generation. That's because these folks, due to the time and culture they were raised in, aren't going to approach problems and challenges in the same way. That shouldn't be a problem for you or them, but it may require you to give way once in a while.

That's because generation Y, for all its glory, can be a bit headstrong. While it's true that you are in many ways more aware of the world than we were at your age, there are still some things you can only learn from experience. So, when students I have gotten to know contact me and mention that they're having problems meshing with the new coworkers, I tell them to be more flexible. A lot of the men and women you're going to find in your company have already been in your shoes; by working with them and following some of their advice, your generation can fulfill its potential and be one of the most productive ever.

Suggested Reading List

1 **The Practice of Management**
Peter Drucker. New York: Harper & Row, 1954.

2 **Managing in a Time of Great Change**
Peter Drucker. New York; Truman Tally Books, 1995.

3 **The 22 Immutable Laws of Markting**
Jack Trout and Al Ries. New York; HarperCollins, 1993.

4 **Marketing Warfare**
Jack Trout and Al Ries. New York: McGraw-Hill, 1986.

5 **Hagakure: The Book of the Samurai.**
Translated by William Scott Wilson. New York: Avon Books, 1979

6 **When Executives Burn Out**
Harry Levinson. Harvard Business Review, May-June, 1981.

7 **Work of Craft**
Carla Neeldeman. New York: Alfred A. Knopf, 1979.

8 **The ' Do Right' Rule. Ethics 4 Everyone: The Handbook for Integrity-Based Business Practices**
Cornerstone Leadership Institute. 2002.

9 **Seeds of Change**
Henry Hobhouse. New York: Harper & Row, 1986.

10 **As a Man Thinketh**
James James. Rockville: Arc Manor, 2007.

11 *Think and Grow Rich*
Napolean Hill. New York: Penguin Group, 2005.

12 *Over The Top*
Zig Ziglar. Nashville: Thomas Nelson, Inc., 1994.

13 *Leadership From The Inside Out*
Keven Cashman. Provo: Executive Excellence Publishing, 1998.

14 *Blue Ocean Stragegy*
W. Chan Kim and Renee Mauborgne. Harvard Business School Press, 2005.

15 *The New Rules of Marketing & PR*
David Meerman Scott. Hoboken: John Wiley & Sons, Inc., 2009.

16 *Rules of Thumb*
Alan M. Webber. New York:HarperCollins, 2009

17 *First, Break All The Rules*
Marcus Buckingham and Curt Coffman. New York: Simon & Schuster, 1999.

18 *Waiting for Your Cat to Bark*
Bryan Eisenberg and Jeffrey. Nashville: Nelson Business, 2006.

19 *Good to Great*
Jim Collins. New York: HarperCollins, 2001.

About the Author

Joe Mayne is a professional speaker and author from Minneapolis, Minnesota. For more than 15 years, he's been teaching college students from hundreds of campuses across North America how to stand out in the job search process.

From the beginning of his career, when he was hired by a Fortune 500 firm before he graduated college, Joe has been intrigued by the dynamics of the job hunting process. Later, in his work as a recruiter, manager, and consultant, he conducted thousands of interviews and learned how to evaluate candidates from an employer's perspective. He continues to gather and share those insights today through his books, articles, and keynote speeches.

Joe's articles and e-books have been featured nationally online and in the print media, and he continues to give dozens of presentations to colleges and universities each year.

You can find out more about him and his work at:

www.MayneSpeaker.com

Breinigsville, PA USA
31 August 2009
223232BV00001B/1/P